Turkey Brother

And Other Tales
Iroquois Folk Stories

Turkey Brother

And Other Tales
Iroquois Folk Stories

As Told by Joseph Bruchac
Illustrated by Kahonhes

The
Crossing Press
Trumansburg
New York

1419

Copyright Ⓒ 1975 The Crossing Press

Scolnik Sykes Design
Printed by Hall Printing Company

Library of Congress Cataloging in Publication Data

Bruchac, Joseph, 1942--
    Turkey Brother, and Other Tales.

    (The Crossing Press series of children's stories)
    SUMMARY: A collection of Iroquois legends about
animals and folk heroes.

        1. Iroquois Indians--Legends. [1. Iroquois Indians--
Legends. 2. Indians of North America--Legends.]
I. Ka-Hon-Hes.   II. Title.
E99.I7B87   398.2   75-35580
ISBN 0-912278-68-4

These stories are for Liana, Shaylou, Matoaka and Mahylou—the Grandchildren of Swift Eagle.

Contents

Introduction

These stories, which are so much older than my own voice, are stories which I have told to my own two sons, James and Jesse. Like all stories that I know from Native American traditions they have messages, sometimes very subtle, which can help show young people the good paths to follow. Yet these stories are never moralistic or tiresome in the way that some stories written FOR children can be, perhaps because too many stories written FOR children are actually written AT children.

When Turtle speaks he is still turtle, not just a human being disguised as an animal. He is one of the great tricksters and he also has his lessons to teach us. Sometimes these lessons can be funny and remind us that (just as in the Ghanaian folk tales of Anansi the Spider or the Igbos' Tortoise) just because one is small does not mean that one will always be a loser. If you know how to use your wits, even an animal as big as Bear cannot defeat you. On the other hand, as Turtle's War Party shows us, even a trickster can sometimes be too smart for his own good.

These stories owe a great deal to many people. Several books have been primary sources for me, among them Arthur Parker's "Seneca Myths and Folk Tales" and Jeremiah Curtin and John Hewitt's "Seneca Fiction, Legends and Myths." I would like especially to mention Arthur Parker, a Seneca himself, who never allowed his learning in the schools of White People to stand between himself and the earth. I have seen his medicine bundle in the Six Nations Museum at Onchiota, New York, and heard a story from Ray Fadden, its founder, which make that very clear. I've also referred often to the Bibliography of Iroquoian Literature published by the New York State Museum, a listing which has some errors in it, but is still very useful.

More than anything else, however, these stories that I have told or retold are the result of my friendship with people such as Swift Eagle. By listening to his stories, I have learned the voice with which one must tell the old tales. Swift Eagle has a record which was put out by Caedmon a few years ago. It is called "The Pueblo Indians in Story, Song and Dance" (TC 1327) and anyone who enjoys these stories should buy that record. From Swift Eagle and from his son, Powhatan, I have learned that the voice for a good story must be a voice which does not hurry, a voice which speaks each word slowly, clearly, and as it should be spoken. This is the way I tell these stories to my children and this is the way these stories should be read...and they are written to be read aloud.

Freezing Moon 1974

Joseph Bruchac

12

The Coming of Legends

Long ago, in the days before people told legends, there was a boy who hunted birds. One day he had been hunting for a very long time and, because it was growing dark, he sought shelter near a great rock. As he sat there, chipping at a piece of flint to make an arrowpoint, he heard a deep voice speak.

"I shall tell a story," the voice said.

The boy was startled and he looked all around him, but could find no one. "Who are you?" said the boy.

"I am Hahskwahot," answered the voice. Thus the boy realized that it was the big standing rock which had spoken.

"Then let me hear your story," said the boy.

"First," said the voice of the stone, "You must make me a present of one of the birds you have killed."

"So be it," said the boy, placing a bird on the rock. Then the deep voice told him a story full of wonder, a story of how things were in the former world. When the story was over, the boy went home.

That evening, the boy returned with another bird and, placing it on the rock, sat down to listen.

"Now," said the voice, "I shall tell you a legend. When one is ended, I may tell you another, but if you become sleepy, you must tell me so we can take a rest and you can return the following evening."

Thus it continued. Soon the boy began to bring people with him and together they listened to the legends told by the standing rock. A great many people now went to the place and listened.

Finally, the voice from the rock spoke to the boy who was no longer a boy but now a man. "You will grow old, but you will have these legends to help you in your old age. Now you have become the carrier of these stories of the former world, and you shall be welcomed and fed wherever you go."

And so it was that legends came into the world.

Three Tales about Turtle

Although you would not think it to look at him, Turtle is one of the most clever of the animals and has a very high opinion of himself. Perhaps this is because he knows that the world tree, from whose branches we have all come, grows from the back of a Great Turtle. These are three stories about Turtle, two in which he used his cleverness to beat an enemy, and one in which he allowed his own good opinion of himself to overcome his common sense.

Turtle's Race with Beaver

Turtle lived in a quiet pool in the big Swamp. There were plenty of fish for him to catch and trees lined the edges of his fishing hole. One day the sun was very hot and Turtle grew sleepy. He crawled onto the mud bank at the edge of his pool, made himself comfortable and soon was fast asleep. He must have slept much longer than he intended, for when he woke up something was definitely wrong. There was water all around him and even over his head! He had to swim and swim to reach the surface and, as he poked his head up into the air, he heard a loud, earsplitting WHAP!

Turtle looked around and soon saw another animal swimming toward him. The animal had big front teeth and a large wide tail. "What are you doing in my pond?" Turtle called out to the animal.

"Your pond? This is my pond and I am Beaver! I built that dam over there and made this place."

Turtle looked. It was true, there was a big dam across the stream, and it had been made from many of Turtle's favorite trees which Beaver had cut down with his sharp teeth. Other trees, which Beaver had cut to eat their sweet bark, were lying on their sides all around the pond.

"No," Turtle said, "This was my private fishing pond before you came with your dam. I will break your dam and drive you away."

20

Beaver whistled loudly and slapped the water with his big tail so loudly that Turtle jumped. "Go ahead," Beaver said, "But if you break down my dam, my brothers and my cousins will come back and build it again, and they will gnaw your head off too!"

Turtle began to think. It was obvious that he could not drive Beaver away by force. He would have to use his wits. "I propose we have a contest," Turtle said. "The winner will stay and the loser will go away forever."

"Good," said Beaver, "Let us see who can stay under the water the longest. I will surely win, for I can stay under the water for a year."

Turtle was not pleased to hear that, for he had been planning to propose the same contest and it was obvious now that Beaver could beat him. "No," said Turtle, "That would be too easy a contest for me to win. I have a better idea. We will have a swimming race."

Beaver agreed to that and allowed Turtle to set the course. "We will start from this stump," Turtle said, "And see who can get to the other side of the pond the fastest. In order to make it fair, since I am such a good swimmer, I will start from behind you."

The two of them made ready, and at Turtle's signal began swimming as fast as they could. Beaver was faster than Turtle, but before he could completely outdistance his rival, Turtle stuck out his long neck and grabbed Beaver by the tail with his jaws. This made Beaver very angry, and he swam as fast as he could, hoping to make Turtle let go. When Turtle grabs something with his jaws, though, he does not let go until he is ready and Beaver could not shake him loose.

Finally, determined to shake loose his enemy, Beaver swung his tail over his head, throwing Turtle through the air like a bird. This was just what Turtle had hoped for; he landed far ahead of Beaver and easily reached the finish line first.

Thus Beaver lost the great race with Turtle and had to desert his dam, while Turtle, the crafty one, won back his private fishing hole.

Turtle's Race with Bear

It was an early winter, cold enough so that the ice had frozen on all the ponds and Bear, who had not yet learned in those days that it was wiser to sleep through the White Season, grumbled as he walked through the woods. Perhaps he was remembering a trick another animal had played on him, perhaps he was just not in a good mood. It happened that he came to the edge of a great pond and saw Turtle there with his head sticking out of the ice.

"Hah," shouted Bear, not even giving his old friend a greeting. "What are you looking at, Slow One?"

Turtle looked at Bear. "Why do you call me slow?"

Bear snorted. "You are the slowest of the animals. If I were to race you, I would leave you far behind." Perhaps Bear had never heard of Turtle's big race with Beaver and perhaps Bear was not remembering that Turtle, like Coyote, was an animal whose greatest speed was in his wits. But even if he had remembered, it was too late now. Turtle had been given a chance to make what had been a boring day into an interesting one.

"My friend," Turtle said, "Let us have a race to see who is the swiftest."

"All right," said Bear. "Where will we race?"

"We will race here at this pond and the race will be tomorrow morning when the sun is the width of one hand above the horizon. You will run along the banks of the pond and I will swim in the water."

"How can that be?" Bear said. "There is ice all over the pond."

"We will do it this way," said Turtle. "I will make holes in the ice along the side of the pond and swim under the water to each hole and stick my head out when I reach it."

"I agree," said Bear. "Tomorrow we will race."

When the next day came, many of the other animals had gathered to watch. They lined the banks of the great pond and watched Bear as he rolled in the snow and jumped up and down making himself ready.

Finally, just as the sun was a hand's width in the sky, Turtle's head popped out of the hole in the ice at the starting line. "Bear," he called, "I am ready."

Bear walked quickly to the starting place and as soon as the signal was given, he rushed forward, snow flying from his feet and his breath making great white clouds above his head. Turtle's head disappeared in the first hole and then in almost no time at all reappeared from the next hole, far ahead of Bear.

"Here I am, Bear," Turtle called. "Catch up to me!" And then he was gone again. Bear was astonished and ran even faster. But before he could reach the next hole, he saw Turtle's green head pop out of it.

"Here I am, Bear," Turtle called again. "Catch up to me!" Now bear began to run in earnest. His sides were puffing in and out as he ran and his eyes were becoming bloodshot, but it was no use. Each time, long before he would reach each of the holes, the ugly green head of Turtle would be there ahead of him, calling out to him to catch up!

When Bear finally reached the finish line, he was barely able to crawl. Turtle was waiting there for him, surrounded by all the other animals. Bear had lost the race. He dragged himself home in disgrace, so tired that he fell asleep as soon as he reached his home. He was so tired that he slept until the warm breath of the Spring came to the woods again.

It was not long after Bear and all the other animals had left the pond that Turtle tapped on the ice with one long claw. At his signal a dozen ugly heads just like his popped up from the holes all along the edge of the pond. It was Turtle's cousins and brothers, all of whom looked just like him!

"My relatives," Turtle said, "I wish to thank you. Today we have shown Bear that it does not pay to call other people names. We have taught him a good lesson."

Turtle smiled and a dozen other turtles, all just like him, smiled back. "And we have shown the other animals," Turtle said, "That Turtles are not the slowest of the animals."

Turtle Makes War on Men

One day Turtle decided he would go on the warpath against the Human Beings. He painted his cheeks red and climbed into his canoe, singing a war song. He had not paddled far down the river before he saw a figure standing on the bank. It was Bear.

"Greetings! Thanks be given that you are strong, Little Brother," said Bear. "Where are you going?"

"I am going to make war on the Human Beings," said Turtle. "Too long have they made war on animals. Now is the time for us to strike back."

"Hah!" Bear said, "Perhaps you are right. I would like to go with you."

Turtle looked at the huge form of Bear and at his own small canoe. "What can you do as a warrior?" Turtle quickly asked. "Why should I take you on my war party?"

"I am very big and strong," said Bear. "I can crush an enemy in my arms."

Turtle shook his head and paddled away. "No," he said, "You would be too slow to go on the warpath with me."

After Turtle had gone a few more miles down the stream, he saw another figure waving to him from the banks of the river. He paddled his canoe closer and saw it was Wolf. "Turtle," shouted Wolf, "I hear you are going to make war on Human Beings. You must take me with you!"

Turtle looked at Wolf and at Wolf's long sharp teeth. Wolf was not as big as Bear, but he was still big enough to make Turtle worry if his small canoe could hold so much weight.

"What can you do?" asked Turtle.

"I can run very fast to attack the enemy. With my long teeth I can bite them."

But Turtle was already paddling away down the river. "No," he called back over his shoulder, "You would not do to go with me on my war party. You are too fast and you would run away and leave me behind."

When Turtle had rounded the bend in the river, he saw a strange animal standing on the banks. The animal was no larger than Turtle himself and was wearing a beautiful black and white robe. Turtle pulled his canoe in to the shore.

"You," Turtle said, "Do you want to go with me to make war on Human Beings?"

"That is a good idea," said the strange animal. "I know that with my secret weapon I can be of help."

"What is your secret weapon?" asked Turtle.

"I cannot tell you," said the animal, turning his back towards Turtle, "But I can show you."

The animal, whose name was Skunk, was certainly right. His secret weapon was very powerful and after Turtle had washed himself off in the river, it was agreed that Skunk would accompany Turtle. The two of them set off down the river, only stopping when another strange animal called to them from the forest.

"Take me with you," called the animal. "I wish to make war on the Human Beings also."

"Who are you?" asked Turtle.

"I am Rattlesnake," said the long thin animal. "I have great magic in my long fangs and can kill any animal by touching them. Shall I show you?"

Turtle shook his head quickly, remembering his experience with Skunk. "No," he said, "I believe you. Come into the boat and we will go together and make war. With a war party as powerful as our own, we will soon destroy all of the Human Beings in the world!"

A few miles further on down the river was a small village of the Iroquois. It was there that Turtle decided to make his first raid. The three warriors talked over the strategy and it was decided that surprise attack would be most effective. Skunk hid himself in the bushes near the small spring where the women came each morning to fill their water pots, Snake coiled up in a pile of firewood beside one of the lodges, and Turtle pulled his head and feet into his shell after placing himself next to the overturned cooking pots.

Bright and early the next morning, a woman went to the spring to get water. As soon as she bent over to fill her pot, Skunk shot her with his weapon. This woman was very brave, however, and even though she was coughing and choking, she beat Skunk with her fists until he was almost dead and then staggered back to the village. When Skunk recovered, he crawled away into the bushes, resolving never to attack Human Beings again. Turtle's war party was now down to only two.

Rattlesnake's turn was not far off. A man asked his wife to bring in some wood to start the cooking fire. This woman had very sharp eyes and she saw the telltale coils of Rattlesnake hidden among the logs.

28

Grabbing a handful of stones, she began to hurl them at Rattlesnake and it was all he could do to manage to escape with his life. So many of the stones struck him that his head was flattened out and to this day all Rattlesnakes have a flattened head as a result of Turtle's war party.

Now Turtle was the only warrior left. He bided his time, waiting for a chance to strike. The chance finally came when a man walked over to the cooking pots, intending to pick one up to use for the morning meal. Instead of picking up a pot, he grabbed Turtle who shot his head out of his shell and bit the man firmly on his leg.

"Ow, Ohhh!" shouted the man, "Let go of me." But Turtle would not let go. The man grabbed a big stick and began beating Turtle with it so hard that it cracked Turtle's shell in many places, but still Turtle would not let go.

"I am going to place you in the fire and burn you," panted the man, and this frightened Turtle very much.

"I have not used my wits," thought Turtle and then cried out in a loud boasting voice; "Put me in the fire. It is my home and will make me grow stronger. Only do not put me in the water."

"Ah-hah!" cried the man, "So you are afraid of the water!" He gritted his teeth from the pain and hobbled down to the river where he thrust in his leg with Turtle still holding on firmly. Turtle waited until he was deep enough and then, letting go of the man's leg, he swam away under water as fast as he could.

Ever since that day, even though Turtle still wears the red paint of war on his cheeks, he has avoided Human Beings, his cracked shell a reminder to him of what happened when he decided to make war on People.

How Bear Lost His Tail

Back in the old days, Bear had a tail which was his proudest possession. It was long and black and glossy and Bear used to wave it around just so that people would look at it. Coyote saw this. Coyote, as everyone knows, is a trickster and likes nothing better than fooling others. So it was that he decided to play a trick on Bear.

It was the time of year when Hatho, the Spirit of Frost, had swept across the land, covering the lakes with ice and pounding on the trees with his big hammer. Coyote had cut a hole in the ice, right near a place where Bear liked to walk. All around Coyote, in a big circle, were fish that he had caught, big trout and fat perch. Sure enough, just as he was about to ask Coyote what he was doing, Coyote twitched his tail, which he had sticking through that hole in the ice, and pulled out a huge trout.

"Greetings, Brother," said Coyote. "How are you this fine day?"

"Greetings," answered Bear, looking at the big circle of fat fish.

"I am well, Brother. But what are you doing?"

"I am fishing," answered Coyote. "Would you like to try?"

"Oh, yes," said Bear, as he started to lumber over to Coyote's fishing hole.

But Coyote stopped him. "Wait,Brother," he said. "This place will not be good. As you can see, I have already caught all the fish. Let us make you a new fishing spot where you can catch many big trout."

Bear agreed and so he followed Coyote to the new place, a place where, as Coyote knew very well, the lake was too shallow to catch the winter fish—which always stay in the deepest water when Hatho has covered their ponds. Bear watched as Coyote cut the hole in the ice, already tasting the fine fish he would soon catch. "Now," Coyote said, "You must do just as I tell you. Clear your mind of all thoughts of fish. Do not even think of a song or the fish will hear you. Turn your back to the hole and place your tail inside it. Soon a fish will come and grab your tail and you can pull him out."

"But how will I know if a fish has grabbed my tail if my back is turned?" asked Bear.

"I will hide over here where the fish cannot see me," said Coyote. "When a fish grabs your tail, I will shout. Then you must pull as hard as you can to catch your fish. But you must be very patient. Do not move at all until I tell you."

Bear nodded, "I will do exactly as you say." He sat down next to the hole, placing his long beautiful black tail in the icy water and turning his back.

Coyote watched for a time to make sure that Bear was doing as he was told and then, very quietly, sneaked back to his own house and went to bed. The next morning he woke up and thought of Bear. "I wonder if he is still there," Coyote said to himself. "I'll just go and check."

So Coyote went back to the ice covered pond and what do you think he saw? He saw what looked like a little white hill in the middle of the ice. It had snowed during the night and covered Bear, who had fallen asleep while waiting for Coyote to tell him to pull out his tail and catch a fish. And Bear was snoring. His snores were so loud that the ice was shaking. It was so funny that Coyote rolled with laughter. But when he was through laughing, he decided the time had come to wake up poor Bear. He crept very close to Bear's ear, took a deep breath, and then shouted: "NOW, BEAR!!!"

Bear woke up with a start and pulled his long tail as hard as he could. But his tail had been caught in the ice which had frozen over during the night and as he pulled, it broke off—Whack!—just like that. Bear turned around to look at the fish he had caught and instead saw his long lovely tail caught in the ice.

"Ohhh," he moaned, "Ohhh, Coyote, I will catch you for this." But Coyote, even though he was laughing fit to kill, was still faster than Bear and he leaped aside and was gone.

So it is that even to this day Bears have short tails and no love at all for Coyote. And if you ever hear a Bear moaning, it is probably because he remembers the trick Coyote played on him long ago and he is mourning for his lost tail.

KAHONHES

Battle with the Snakes

There was a man who was not kind to animals. One day when he was hunting, he found a rattlesnake and decided to torture it. He held its head to the ground and pierced it with a piece of bark. Then, as it helplessly was caught there, he tormented it.

"We shall fight," he said and then burned the snake until it was dead. He thought this was a great jest and so, whenever he found a snake, he would do the same thing again.

One day, however, another man from his village was walking through the forest when he heard a strange sound. It was louder than the wind hissing through the tops of tall pine trees and he crept closer to see. There, in a great clearing, were many snakes. They were gathered for a war council and as he listened in fright he heard them say:

"We shall now fight with them. Djisdaah has challenged us and we shall go to war. In four days we shall go their village and fight them."

The man crept away and then ran as fast as he could to his village to tell what he had heard and seen. Others were sent by the chief to see if his words were true and they returned in great fright.

"Ahhhh," they said, "It is so. The snakes are all gathering to have a war."

The chief of the village could see that he had no choice. "We must fight," he said and then ordered the people of the village to make preparations for the battle. They cut mountains of wood and stacked it in long piles all around the village. They built rows of stakes close together to keep the snakes out. When the fourth day came, the chief ordered that the piles of wood be set on fire and just as he did so they heard a great noise, a noise like a great wind in the trees. It was the noise of the snakes, hissing as they came to the village to do battle.

Usually a snake will not go near a fire, but these snakes were determined to have their revenge. They went straight into the flames and many of them died. But the living snakes crawled over the bodies of the dead ones and in spite of the battle given them by the people of the village, they continued to move forward until they reached the second row of stakes.

Once again, the chief ordered that the piles of wood in the second row of defense be set on fire and it was done. But the snakes crawled straight into the flames, hissing their war songs, and the living crawled over the bodies of the dead. It was a terrible sight. Now they had reached the second row of stakes and even though the people fought bravely, it was no use. The snakes were more numerous than fallen leaves and they could not be stopped. Soon they had forced their way past the last row of stakes and the people of the village were fighting for their lives. The first man to be killed was Djisdaah, the one who had challenged the snakes to battle.

It was now clear that they could never win this battle and the chief of the village shouted to the snakes, who had reached the edge of the village: "Hear me, my brothers. We surrender to you. We have done you a great wrong. Have mercy on us."

All of the snakes stopped where they were and there was a great silence. The exhausted warriors looked at the great army of snakes and the snakes stared back at them. Then the earth trembled and cracked in front of the human beings. A great snake, a snake taller than the biggest pine tree, whose head was larger than a great longhouse, lifted himself out of the hole in the earth.

"Hear me," he said. "I am the chief of all the snakes. We shall go and leave you in peace if you will agree to two things."

The chief looked at the great snake and nodded his head. "We will agree, Great Chief," he said.

"It is well," said the Chief of the Snakes. "These are the two things. First, you must always treat my people with respect. Secondly, as long as the world stands, you will never name another man Djisdaah."

And so it was agreed and so it is, even until today.

Two Feathers and Turkey Brother

Many seasons ago an old man lived with his two nephews deep in a forest. One of the boys was almost grown to manhood and the other, who followed his brother everywhere, was only a little boy. One day the uncle went hunting and brought home a big white turkey.

"My Uncle," begged the little brother, "please make a costume for me from the skin of the turkey."

So the uncle carefully skinned out the turkey and made it into a costume for the little brother. And the little brother put his legs into the legs of the turkey, he put his arms into the turkey's wings and then...ahh-ahhh, he looked just like a turkey. Not only that, he could fly like one! He was so happy with his costume that he never took it off and so his older brother gave him a new name. "From now on," said the older brother, "We will call you Turkey Brother."

Meanwhile, the uncle who had been watching the boys very closely for a long time came to a decision and called the older brother to him. "My Nephew, the time has come for you to become a man. There are things which you must do. But first you must build a sweat lodge and purify yourself. There in the sweat lodge you must fast and wait for your protectors to appear to you."

The nephew did as his uncle told him. He left the house of his uncle and went to the river where he built a sweat lodge. For many days he fasted and prayed. Finally, when he was so weak he could barely lift his head, a great spider appeared to him, as if in a dream. "I am your guardian," said the Spider as it wove its web down towards him, "Call on me when you need help." And then it was gone.

Once again he had a dream. And in this dream he saw a great Blacksnake lifting itself above the trees. "I am your strong protector," said the Blacksnake, as it lowered its tail towards him. "Call on me when you are in great trouble." And then it was gone.

When the older brother returned to the house of his uncle and told him of his visions, the old man was overjoyed. "The time has come," he said. "Long ago evil sorcerers killed your parents and I fled with you to this place in the forest. But now the time has come for you to return to the land of your parents. First, however, I must give you clothing which will be right for you."

Then the old man unrolled a bundle and took from it a robe made of raccoon skins. The older brother put it on and thought it was a very fine robe. "No," said the uncle, "That is not good enough."

Then the old man unrolled another bundle and brought out a robe made of the skins of wildcats. The older brother put it on and thought it too to be a very fine robe. "No," said the uncle, "That is not good enough."

Then the old man unrolled another bundle and brought out a robe made of the skin of a mountain lion. The animal's head was the cap and on top of the cap were two loon feathers which began to sing as soon as the older brother put the robe on. The older brother was greatly pleased and so was the uncle. "Now," said the old man, "When people see you in this, they will know your true worth. Among the people there is a chief who has two daughters and one of them should be your wife."

Then the old man gave other gifts to his nephew. He gave him a bow and arrows and a great war club. He gave him beautiful moccasins and leggings to match. And lastly, he gave him a pouch which was made out of the skin of a fisher. If anyone ever tried to reach into that pouch through the mouth, which was also the mouth of the animal, then the pouch would bite him. Only Two Feathers, the older brother, could reach into that pouch without getting bitten. In that pouch was a marvelous stone pipe. The bowl was carved to resemble a bullfrog and the stem a water snake and whenever it was smoked, the snake would try to swallow the frog and the frog would croak.

The time had now come for Two Feathers to leave, but Turkey Brother would not allow him to go. He begged so piteously to go with him that finally the uncle relented.

"Go with your older brother," said the uncle, "But before you leave, I have words of warning for both of you. Your journey is long. You must travel towards the west, a six years' journey. Along the way there are many dangers. If you should see a very small boy standing under a tree, pass by him quickly. He is the servant of a witch and he will ask you to lift him to your shoulders so that he can climb into the tree. If you do that, you will be carried through the air and dropped through the smoke hole of the witch's lodge and land in her fire. There is also a very dangerous spring along the way. It is close to the path, but you must not drink from it or touch the water. Finally, when you are within sight of the village you are travelling to, you will see an old man dancing strangely around a big tree. Pay no attention to him, for he is a dangerous sorcerer."

The next morning came and Two Feathers and Turkey Brother started on their journey, Two Feathers striding along the path and Turkey Brother flying over his head. It was a fine day and they travelled quickly. By the time it was noon they had travelled as far as an ordinary person would travel in two years. They had stopped to rest for a short while when they heard a small voice.

"Uncle," called the small voice, "Please lift me up. I cannot reach the branches of this tree."

There in front of them was a very small boy standing under a hemlock tree. Turkey Brother flew up into the branches and flapped his wings. "Brother, do not touch the boy. Remember the words of our uncle."

But Two Feathers strode up to the very small boy, picked him up... and instead of placing him on his own shoulders put him on top of a large stump. As soon as he had done so, the boy vanished and two long arms came out of the sky, plucked the stump out of the ground and carried it away to drop it through the smoke hole of the witch's lodge. When the stump fell through the smoke hole, it knocked the astonished witch into the fire.

Now that they were rested, Two Feathers and Turkey Brother set forth again on their journey. Once again they traveled quickly and when

42

the end of the day was coming they found themselves standing near a beautiful spring.

Turkey Brother flew up into the branches of a beech tree. "Brother," he called down, "Be careful. This is surely the spring our Uncle warned us about."

But Two Feathers strode up to the spring. He knelt beside it and bent over to have a drink. But just as his lips were touching the water... two big hands reached up and grabbed him to pull him down into the spring. However, Two Feathers was too strong and he reached down into the water with his own hands and pulled out a very strange creature. It was all covered with hair and was as large as a man. "Grandson," it squeaked, "Put me back. I will not harm you."

But Two Feathers paid no attention to its cries. He gave his war club to Turkey Brother and told him to guard the creature. Then he returned to the spring and bent once more to drink. Once more two big hands grabbed at him and once more Two Feathers reached down and pulled another monster from the water.

"Grandson," it cried, "Do not harm me. Put me back."

But Two Feathers did not listen to it. He threw it on the bank with the other creature and told Turkey Brother to guard it. Then he bent again to drink. The water was sweet and pure. Then he and Turkey Brother burned the two creatures which had lived in that spring for many years, drowning unsuspecting travellers who bent down to drink.

The two brothers spent the night in that place and the next morning they started out again on their journey. They travelled well and by the time it was late afternoon they were within sight of the village their uncle had told them of. But there in front of them was a big tree and around it danced a strange old man wearing dirty and ragged clothes.

Turkey Brother grew frightened and flew up into the limbs of a beech tree.

"Brother," he called down, "Beware. This is surely the old man our Uncle warned us of."

Just then the old man turned around.

"Grandson," called the dirty old man to Two Feathers, "Help me catch that raccoon in the top of this tree."

Two Feathers looked up and sure enough, there was a fat raccoon in the top of the tree.

"Shoot him with your arrow, Grandson," said the old man. Two Feathers lifted his bow, ignoring the cries of Turkey Brother, who was flapping his wings in distress from the beech tree, and shot at the raccoon. His arrow struck it and it fell into the hollow near the top of the tree. "Climb up and get him, Grandson," said the old man, "But first take off your fine clothing so that it will not catch on the tree as you climb."

Two Feathers took off his beautiful robe and his fisher pouch, he took off his moccasins and leggings, he put down his club and his bow and arrows and he climbed the tree. He climbed and he climbed until he reached the hollow where the raccoon had fallen into the tree. He reached in to look for the raccoon and then, before he knew it, he found himself falling into the tree and all was darkness.

At the base of the tree the old man laughed. He took off his dirty ragged clothing and put on the fine clothes of Two Feathers. Now he no longer looked like an old man. Because of the magic of the mountain lion skin, he looked like a fine young warrior. He tried to pick up the bow and arrow so that he could shoot poor Turkey Brother, who was flapping his wings in dismay from the beech tree, but he found that he could not lift the bow of Two Feathers from the ground. Hah, it did not matter. He left them where they were and strode off towards the village.

When Two Feathers woke, he found himself in a very terrible place. All around him were the bones of human beings. He tried to climb out, but the sides were too slippery and he fell back each time he tried. At last he sat down and closed his eyes. "My Protector," he said, "I need your help."

Then, as if in a dream, a great Spider appeared and wove a web down to him. Two Feathers began to climb the web, but it broke and he fell back into the terrible place.

Again he sat and closed his eyes. "My Guardian," he said, "I am in need of you." Then, as if in a dream, he saw the great Blacksnake. It lowered its tail to him and he reached out to grasp it. It lifted him to safety.

When Two Feathers reached the bottom of the tree, he found Turkey Brother waiting for him with his bow and arrows. Turkey Brother helped him put on the dirty torn clothing of the old man, and now Two Feathers looked like an old, old man. Turkey Brother was greatly distressed, but Two Feathers calmed him. "Let us continue to the village," he said, and they began walking very slowly in the direction in which the old man had gone.

By now the old man who was wearing the robe of Two Feathers had reached the village. The first person he met was the oldest

daughter of the chief who thought the old man was indeed a hand-
some young warrior. "Come to my lodge," she said. "I wish to make
you my husband." And so it was that the old man who had stolen
the robe of Two Feathers came in honor to the lodge of the chief
and ate marriage bread.

It was almost dark when Two Feathers and Turkey Brother reached
the stream near the village. There they met the youngest daughter of the
chief who had come to get water. "Who are you?" she said to the strange
pair.

"We are two brothers," Two Feathers said. "We have travelled many
miles to come here and have had many adventures." Then he told her of
all that had befallen them.

"Now," Two Feathers said, "I have come to this village to seek a
wife." The youngest daughter of the chief looked at the old man. She
looked beyond the dirty, torn clothing he was wearing and looked into
his eyes. And something went out from his eyes into hers. "You do not
have to seek further," she said. "I wish to make you my husband."

So it was that Two Feathers, wearing the dirty torn clothing of the
old man also came to the lodge of the chief and ate marriage bread with
Drooping Flower, the youngest daughter of the chief.

Although everyone had welcomed the fine warrior who had
married the oldest daughter of the chief, they did not give the same
welcome to Two Feathers, who seemed to be a very old, very dirty
person. Only the chief did not object. "My daughter knows her own
mind," he said and that was all.

That night the old man who was wearing the robe of Two
Feathers would not take off his clothes, for fear that Two Feathers

would take them back. And when he reached into the pouch to take out the fine pipe he saw in the bottom of it, the fisher's head bit him savagely and he had to pry his hand loose. He took the pouch from his belt and threw it out of the lodge where Two Feathers found it and picked it up. Then, before going to bed, Two Feathers took out the magic pipe and smoked it. When he did so, the bullfrog croaked and the snake on the stem tried to catch it, and everyone was amazed and began to think better of the old dirty man the youngest daughter had married.

The next day Two Feathers called his wife to him. "Bring a wooden bowl to me," he said. Drooping Flower did so and, as she watched, Two Feathers spat wampum into the bowl until it was filled with black wampum. "Take this to your father," he said. Drooping Flower did so and her father was very pleased.

But the wife of the old man who was wearing the robe of Two Feathers was not happy. "Look," she said to her husband, "Can you do this too?"

"Of course," boasted the old man. "Bring me your father's best wooden bowl." The daughter did so and then the old man spat into it. But he did not spit wampum. Instead he spat up dead and half-decayed worms and lizards. "Take that to your father," he said proudly.

The daughter did so and her father grew very angry. "Take the bowl and burn it," he said in disgust, and the daughter withdrew in disgrace.

On the following day the chief asked his two new sons to go and hunt for him. Two Feathers took his bow and arrows and brought back many fine deer. But all that the old man who had stolen the clothes of

Two Feathers could catch was one old slow woodchuck which he beat to death with a stick. The deer which had been caught by Two Feathers were prepared and everyone ate, especially the old man who was wearing the robe of Two Feathers. The old man ate so much that he became very sleepy. He ate so much that the robe of Two Feathers seemed very tight to him. He crawled off to bed and took off all of the clothing he had stolen before he went to sleep.

Turkey Brother flew up to the smokehole and looked down on the old man who was asleep. He saw all of his brother's fine clothes, which were now torn and dirty, lying beside the old man. "Brother," he called down, "Come and take back the things which are your own."

Then Two Feathers went and took back his robe, his leggings, and his moccasins. And when he put them on, they became new again. When he put them on, he no longer looked like an old man. Now he looked like the fine young warrior he really was. And everyone, except for the chief and his youngest daughter, was greatly surprised to see that the old man was really a fine young warrior.

When the old man finally woke, he found his own clothing lying beside him. He put it on and went outside to find the whole village waiting for him to denounce him. With rocks and clubs he was driven from the village and never seen again.

Two Feathers and Turkey Brother were very happy with the people of the village. Before long, Turkey Brother also came of age and he took a wife. Then the two brothers led the people of the village to the land of their uncle where there was good land and much game. And in that place, reunited with their uncle, all of them lived happily for many years.

The Boy Who Lived With The Bears

There was once a boy whose father and mother had died and so he was left alone in the world. The only person he had to take care of him was his uncle, but his uncle was not a kind man. The uncle thought that the boy was too much trouble and so fed him only the scraps from the table and dressed him in tattered clothing and moccasins whose soles were worn away.When the boy slept at night, he had to sleep outside his uncle's lodge far away from the fire. But the boy never complained because his parents had told him always to respect people older than himself.

One day the uncle decided to get rid of the boy. "Come with me," he said, "We are going hunting. The boy was very happy. His uncle had never taken him hunting before. He followed him into the woods. First his uncle killed a rabbit. The boy picked it up to carry it for the uncle and was ready to turn back to the lodge, but his uncle shook his head. "We will go on. I am not done hunting."

They went further and the uncle killed a fat grouse. The boy was very happy, for they would have so much to eat that surely his uncle would feed him well that night and he began to turn back, but the uncle shook his head again. "No," he said, "We must go on."

Finally, they came to a place very, very far in the forest where the boy had not been before. There was a great cliff and at its base a cave led into the rock. The opening to the cave was large enough only for a small person to go into. "There are animals hiding in there," the uncle said. "You must crawl in and chase them out so that I can shoot them with my arrows."

The cave was very dark and it looked cold inside, but the boy remembered what his parents had taught him. He crawled into the cave. There were leaves and stones, but there were no animals. He reached the very end of the cave and turned back, ashamed that he had not fulfilled his uncle's expectations. And do you know what he saw? He saw his uncle rolling a great stone in front of the mouth of the cave. And then everything was dark.

The boy tried to move the stone, but it was no use. He was trapped! At first he was afraid, but then he remembered what his parents had told him. The orenda of those who are good at heart is very strong. If you do good and have faith, good things will come to you. This made the boy happy and he began to sing a song. The song was about himself, a boy who had no parents and needed friends. As he sang, his song grew louder, until he forgot he was trapped in a cave. But then he heard a scratching noise outside and stopped singing, thinking his uncle had come back to let him out of the cave.

However, as soon as he heard the first of many voices outside his cave, he knew that he was wrong. That high squeaking voice was not the voice of his uncle. "We should help this boy," said the high squeaking voice.

"Yes," said a very deep voice which sounded warm and loving. "He is all alone and needs help. There is no doubt that we should help him."

"One of us," said another voice, "Will have to adopt him."

And then many other voices, voices of all kinds which seemed to speak in many languages agreed. The strange thing was that the boy could understand all these voices, strange as they were. Then the stone began to move and light streamed into the cave, blinding the boy who had been in the darkness for a long time. He crawled out, very stiff and cold, and looked around him. He was surrounded by many animals!

"Now that we have rescued you," said a small voice from near his feet, "You must choose which of us will be your parents now." He looked down and saw that the one who was speaking was a mole.

"Yes," said a great moose standing in the trees., "You must choose one of us."

"Thank you," said the boy. "You are all so kind. But how can I choose which one of you will be my parents?"

"I know," said the mole. "Let us all tell him what we are like and what kind of lives we lead and then he can decide." There was general agreement on that, and so the animals began to come up to the boy one by one.

"I'll begin," said the mole. "I live under the earth and dig my tunnels through the Earth Mother. It is very dark and cozy in my tunnels and we have plenty of worms and grubs to eat."

"That sounds very good," said the boy. "But I am afraid that I am too big to go into your tunnels, friend Mole."

"Come and live with me," said the Beaver. "I live in a fine lodge in the midst of a pond. We Beavers eat the best bark from the sweetest trees and we dive under the water and sleep in our lodge in the winter time."

"Your life is very interesting too," said the boy, "But I cannot eat bark, and I know that I would freeze in the cold waters of your pond."

"How about me," said the wolf. "I run through the woods and fields and I catch all the small animals I want to eat. I live in a warm den and you would do well to come with me."

"You too are very kind," said the boy, "But all of the animals have been so kind to me, that I would not feel right eating them."

"You could be my child," said the deer. "Run with us through the forest and eat the twigs of the trees and the grass of the fields."

"No, friend Deer," the boy said, "You are beautiful and good, but you are so fast, that I would be left far behind you."

Then an old Bear-woman walked over to the boy. She looked at him a long time before she talked and when she spoke, her voice was like a growling song. "You can come with us and be a Bear," she said. "We bears move slowly and speak with harsh voices, but our hearts are warm. We eat the berries and the roots which grow in the forest and our fur would keep you warm in the long season of cold."

"Yes," said the boy, "I would like to be a Bear. I will come with you and you will be my family." So the boy who had no family went to live with the Bears. The mother bear had two other children and they became brothers to the boy. They would roll and play together and

54

soon the boy was almost as strong as a bear.

"Be careful, though," the old Bear-woman cautioned him. "Your brothers' claws are sharp and wherever they scratch you, you will grow hair just like them." They lived together a long time in the forest and the old Bear-woman taught the boy many things.

One day they were all in the forest seeking berries when the Bear-woman motioned them to silence. "Listen," she said, "There is a hunter." They listened and, sure enough, they heard the sounds of a man walking. The old Bear-woman smiled. "We have nothing to fear from him," she said, "He is the heavy-stepper and the twigs and the leaves of the forest speak of him wherever he goes."

Another time as they walked along, the old Bear-woman again motioned them to silence. "Listen," she said, "Another hunter." They listened and soon they heard the sound of singing. The old Bear-woman smiled. "That one too is not dangerous. He is the flapping-mouth, the one who talks as he hunts and does not remember that everything in the forest has ears. We bears can hear singing even if it is only thought, and not spoken."

So they lived on happily until one day when the old Bear-woman motioned them to silence, a frightened look in her eyes. "Listen," she said, "The one who hunts on two-legs and four-legs. This one is very dangerous to us, and we must hope he does not find us, for the four-legs who hunts with him can follow our tracks wherever we go and the Man himself does not give up until he has caught whatever it is that he is hunting for."

Just then they heard the sound of a dog barking. "Run for your lives," cried the old Bear-woman. "The four-legs has caught our scent."

And so they ran, the boy and the three bears. They ran across streams and up hills, but still the sound of the dog followed them. They ran through swamps and thickets, but the hunters were still close behind. They crossed ravines and forced their way through patches of thorns, but could not escape the sounds of pursuit. Finally, their hearts ready to burst from exhaustion, the old Bear-woman and the boy and the two Bear-brothers came to a great hollow log. "It is our last hope," said the old Bear-woman. "Go inside."

They crawled into the log and waited, panting and afraid. For a time, there was no sound and then the noise of the dog sniffing at the end of their log came to their ears. The old Bear-woman growled and the dog did not dare to come in after them. Then, once again, things were quiet and the boy began to hope that his family would be safe, but his hopes were quickly shattered when he smelled smoke. The resourceful hunter had piled branches at the end of the end of the log and was going to smoke them out!

"Wait," cried the boy in a loud voice. "Do not harm my friends."

"Who is speaking?" shouted a familiar voice from outside the log. "Is there a human being inside there?" There came the sound of branches being kicked away from the mouth of the log and then the smoke stopped. The boy crawled out and looked into the face of the hunter—it was his Uncle!!

"My nephew!" cried the Uncle with tears in his eyes. "Is it truly you? I came back to the cave where I left you, realizing that I had been a cruel and foolish man...but you were gone and there were only the tracks of many animals. I thought they had killed you."

And it was true. Before the Uncle had reached home, he had realized that he had been a wicked person. He had turned back, resolved to treat the son of his own sister well from then on. His grief had truly been great when he had found him gone.

"It is me," said the boy. "I have been cared for by the Bears. They are like my family now, Uncle. Please do not harm them."

The uncle tied his hunting dog to a tree as he nodded his agreement. "Bring out your friends. I will always be the friend of bears from now on if what you say is true."

Uncertain and still somewhat afraid, the old Bear-woman and her two sons came out of the log. They talked to the boy with words which sounded to the uncle like nothing more than animals growling and told him that he must now be a human being again. "We will always be your friends," said the old Bear-woman and she shuffled into the forest after her two sons. "And you will remember what it is to know the warmth of an animal's heart."

And so the boy returned to live a long and happy life with his uncle, a friend to the Bears and all the animals for as long as he lived.

The Porcupine Clan

After a long war between two clans, a lonely man was fleeing through the deep woods. He was the only survivor of one of the clans and he was in fear for his life. Seeing a deep cavern in a rocky cliff, he slipped into it and escaped his pursuers. Far into the darkness he walked until he saw an opening before him. There, in the midst of a wide field, was a lodge. Concealing himself, he watched the lodge and soon saw two women come out. They walked in a strange way and as the man observed their splay-footed way of walking, he knew that they were animal people wearing human forms. They came almost to the place where the man was hiding and then stopped.

"Let us go back," said the younger of the two women, "For I smell something." Then they walked back to the lodge and went inside. Before long, a man came out. He shook himself as a dog shakes upon coming out of the water. All the air about him seemed filled with light for a moment and it was then that the fugitive knew he was watching Porcupine people, those who wear rays of the sun on their backs.

After shaking himself, the man walked close to the place where the fugitive was hiding and then returned to the lodge where he told the two women that they had smelled the scent of a human being. This time when the two women came forth, they walked right to the place where the man was hiding. "Tell us," said the elder of the two, "Why have you come here, Human Being?"

"I came to escape from my enemies," said the man. "All of my people have been killed."

"Ah," said the older woman. "We invite you to our home. Will you come with us?"

"I thank you," said the man. "I will come with you."

So it was that the man came to the lodge of the Porcupine people. Before long, it became obvious that there was affection between him and the younger of the sisters. "Do you wish to marry my sister?" said the Porcupine man. "I shall give her to you and you shall continue to stay with us." Thus it was done.

A year passed and the bridegroom and his wife were blessed with a son. Another year came and with it another child. Thus the time went by and the man found himself the father of many interesting children. It was now twelve years since he had first come to the place, and his brother-in-law called him aside.

"The time has come when you must leave us," said the Porcupine. "You shall take your wife and children and return to the land of the Human Beings. They are your people now, even though they are of our blood also."

The man packed the few belongings he had and with his wife and children made the journey through the cave. They passed through the deep forest and came at last to a place where he had never been before. There he began to hunt, using the many things he had learned from his stay among the Porcupines.

He met other hunters and invited them to his camp where he introduced them to his wife and children. The people marvelled at the strong, well-fed children and at the language they had never heard before which the wife spoke to her offspring. "Of what clan are you?" a man finally asked.

"We are the Wan'dat people and our clan is the Porcupine clan," said the hunter.

So it was that the Porcupine clan became a part of the clans of the Iroquois. They brought with them the knowledge of the omens of the seasons and showed the people many things about gathering food, and they always knew where the pigeons would roost in flocks of thousands. It was from the Porcupine people that the Iroquois learned that the winters would be severe if the bears made their winter quarters early in the fall, and it was from the Porcupines that they learned that seeing a rock damp from the moisture in the air would mean that it would rain the next day. These were only a few of the signs which the Porcupine clan taught to their friends, and it was for these things that the Porcupine clan of the Wan'dat people gained great fame for wisdom.

   Joseph Bruchac lives in Greenfield Center, New York, near Saratoga Springs, a sacred place of healing for the Mohawk people. Part Slovak and part Abnaki, he began hearing the stories collected in this book when he was a small child and has retold them many times since to his own two sons, James and Jesse. A poet and novelist, he won a NYS CAPS award for his writing in 1974 and a National Endowment Fellowship in 1975.

Kahonhes

John Fadden, Kahonhes, who illustrated this book, is an Akwesasne Indian, living on St. Regis Reservation. He is a contributing artist to Akwesasne Notes, and has produced illustrations for the Six Nations Indian Museum, Collier-MacMillan, Ltd., and the National Film Board of Canada.